GUATEMALA

by Joanna J. Robinson

The Child's World

Published by The Child's World®
1980 Lookout Drive • Mankato, MN 56003-1705
800-599-READ • www.childsworld.com

Acknowledgments
The Child's World®: Mary Berendes, Publishing Director
Red Line Editorial: Editorial direction
The Design Lab: Design
Amnet: Production

Design elements: Shutterstock Images
Photographs ©: Shutterstock Images, cover (left top), cover
(left center), cover (left bottom), 1 (top), 1 (bottom left), 1
(bottom right), 17 (left), 17 (right), 27, 28; Sam Chadwick/
Shutterstock Images, cover (right); iStockphoto, 5, 6–7, 8,
11, 18, 21, 22–23, 29; Simon Dannhauer/iStockphoto,
10; Chepe Nicoli/iStockphoto, 12; RJ Lerich/Shutterstock
Images, 13; Ed Fuentesg/iStockphoto, 15; Vladimir
Korostyshevskiy/Shutterstock Images, 16; Micky Wiswedel/
iStockphoto, 20; Paco Romero/iStockphoto, 24, 30; David
Parsons/iStockphoto, 25; Stefano Ember/Shutterstock
Images, 26

ISBN 9781634070461
LCCN 2014959737

Printed in the United States of America
PA02345

ABOUT THE AUTHOR

Joanna J. Robinson is a creative educational writer. She has a passion for providing fun learning materials for children of all ages. Robinson has written educational content and more than 100 original stories. Trips to Mexico, Italy, England, Canada, and Egypt inspire Robinson to share her experiences with young readers.

ONE WORLD · COUNTRIES

GUATEMALA
Q 0.05

TABLE OF CONTENTS

CHAPTER 1

WELCOME TO GUATEMALA! 5

CHAPTER 2

THE LAND 8

CHAPTER 3

GOVERNMENT AND CITIES 13

CHAPTER 4

PEOPLE AND CULTURES 20

CHAPTER 5

DAILY LIFE 25

FAST FACTS, 30

GLOSSARY, 31

TO LEARN MORE, 32

INDEX, 32

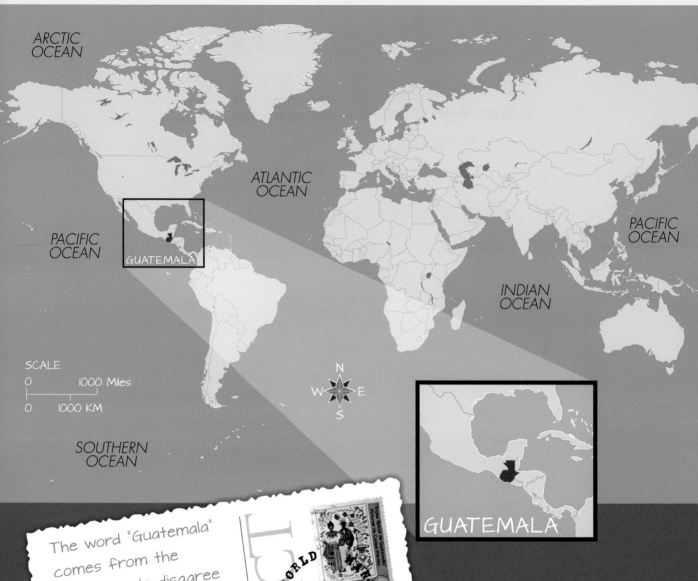

ARCTIC
OCEAN

ATLANTIC
OCEAN

PACIFIC
OCEAN

GUATEMALA

PACIFIC
OCEAN

INDIAN
OCEAN

SCALE
0   1000 Miles
0   1000 KM

N
W   E
S

SOUTHERN
OCEAN

GUATEMALA

FUN FACT

ONE WORLD · MANY COUNTRIES

The word "Guatemala" comes from the Maya. People disagree about what it means. Some think it means "land of trees." Other people believe it means "mountain of vomiting water." This refers to Guatemala's many volcanoes.

CHAPTER 1

WELCOME TO GUATEMALA!

High in the mountains of Guatemala, the sun rises above the peaks. Buildings with red tile roofs are hidden in the morning mist. People are up early, walking down narrow stone streets. They are headed to the market.

The market of Chichicastenango has been set up every week for more than 300 years. The ancient Maya first met there to trade goods. It is still a busy place today.

A woman shows off her sewing work at the Chichicastenango Market.

The goods sold at the market today are not much different than they were in the past. The market is known for its handmade Maya items, such as the *huipil*. This is a woman's shirt woven by hand on a loom. The neck and shoulders often have brightly colored flowers or other designs.

Picnic tables are in the market. People often stop to eat lunch while they shop. People can buy fresh corn tortillas. They may eat their tortillas with *pepian*. It is a thick Maya stew flavored with pumpkin seeds and green salsa.

The influence of the Maya is strong in Guatemala. Maya people make up about half of the country's population. They were the first people to settle in the area. Later, people from Spain arrived in Guatemala. Today, the country is a blend of these two cultures.

A Guatemalan woman makes fresh tortillas at Chichicastenango Market.

THE LAND

Two volcanoes rise above the town of Antigua, Guatemala.

Guatemala is in Central America. Mexico is to the north and west of Guatemala. Belize, Honduras, and the Caribbean Sea form Guatemala's eastern border. El Salvador and the Pacific Ocean are to the south.

The land along the Pacific Ocean is low and flat. The rich soil in this area is Guatemala's most valuable natural resource. It has become an important farming area. Approximately 75 percent of Guatemalans live in this part of the country.

The plains along the coast slowly rise to mountains. Guatemala's mountains have 27 volcanoes. Three of them are active. In 2010, the Santa María volcano erupted. Ash fell on Guatemala City, and people had to leave the city.

North of Guatemala City is Lake Petén Itzá. It covers 40 square miles (100 sq km) and is 165 feet (50 m) deep. Cities dot the land around the lake. Farmers in the area grow crops such as cacao, sugarcane, and fruit.

The temperatures in Guatemala are mild all year. Guatemala has two seasons. The dry season is from November to April. In those months, there is little rainfall. The wet season is from May to October. Heavy rains fall each afternoon and evening.

Rain forests grow well in Guatemala's climate. In 1990, Guatemala's government created the Maya Biosphere Reserve. It is the largest rain forest in Central America. The reserve protects the plants and animals that live there.

Guatemala's warm, wet weather allows a large variety of plants to grow well there.

The rain forest has a great variety of living creatures. Jaguars, howler monkeys, and macaws all live in the rain forest. Leaf-cutter ants, poison dart frogs, and monarch butterflies live there, too. Some of the rain forest's plants include the wild orchards, kapok trees, and açaí palms.

For many years, people cut down trees in the rain forest to make room for farm fields. Animals began losing their homes. Tree roots no longer held soil in place, and it began to erode.

The rain forest is thick with plants, vines, and trees.

The machines people used to cut down the trees created pollution. The rain forest was in danger. Today, laws stop people from cutting down trees in protected areas.

Guatemala's national symbol is the quetzal bird. This small bird has a red throat and green body. The quetzal is rare. The ancient Maya used the quetzal's feathers as money. Today, Guatemala's money is called the quetzal in honor of this tradition.

FUN FACT

ONE WORLD MANY COUNTRIES

GUATEMALA Q.0.05 aéreo

CHAPTER 3

GOVERNMENT AND CITIES

— The National Palace is in Guatemala City.

Guatemala's official name is the **Republic** of Guatemala. It is divided into 22 departments. The departments are similar to states. Each department has a governor. The president chooses the governors for the departments.

Guatemala's president leads the government. The president also meets with world leaders to solve problems. Guatemalans elect a president every four years. They also elect lawmakers. The group of lawmakers is called the Congress of the Republic.

The government meets in Guatemala City. It is the country's capital. It is also the largest city in Central America. About 1.2 million people live there. They call their city by the nickname "Guate."

Guate is divided into 21 *zonas*. Each *zona* is similar to a neighborhood. *Zona* 1 is the historic area of the city. It has churches, **plazas**, theaters, and homes that are more than 200 years old. *Zona* 4 is where all the government buildings are located. *Zonas* 9 and 10 have lots of entertainment. There are museums, gardens, hotels, and restaurants.

Tikal is another important city in Guatemala. It was built by the ancient Maya. They were the first people to live in

The skyline and mountains of Guatemala City

Guatemala. They built many different buildings in Tikal. It has temples, palaces, roads, markets, and carved statues.

Today, no one lives in Tikal. The Maya abandoned it 1,000 years ago. Plants in the rain forest began to grow over the buildings. Over time, the city became completely covered. In the 1950s, scientists began to uncover the buildings. They are now part of Tikal National Park.

An ancient Mayan pyramid in Tikal National Park

Many people travel to Guatemala to visit sites such as Tikal. **Tourism** is an important part of Guatemala's **economy**. Farming is another important part. Many Guatemalans work on farms. They grow coffee beans, sugar, and bananas. Sometimes children also work on farms. They help their families earn money.

The crops grown on farms are used in trade. Guatemala **exports** many of its crops. Guatemala also **imports** many goods, such as fuel, machines, grain, and fertilizers.

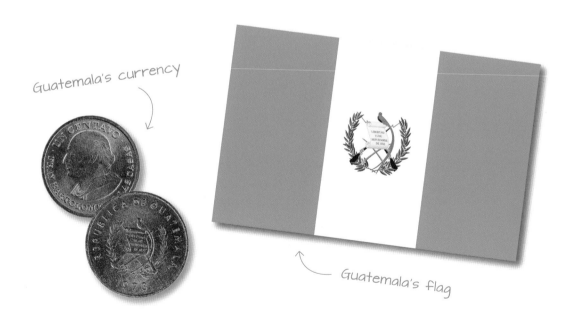

Guatemala's currency

Guatemala's flag

Guatemalan farms use many of these imports. Guatemala's most important trading partners are the United States, El Salvador, China, and Mexico.

FUN FACT

ONE WORLD MANY COUNTRIES

GUATEMALA Q 0.05 aéreo

Guatemala produces more jade than any other country in the world. Jade is a green mineral. It is often polished and made into jewelry or sculptures. Guatemala's jade comes from the Motagua Valley. It is in the center of the country.

GLOBAL CONNECTIONS

Life in Guatemala is not easy. Its past has been filled with fighting and poverty. Between 1960 and 1996, the Guatemalans fought a **civil war**. During those 36 years, thousands of Guatemalans left their country. They wanted to live in peace.

Guatemala's **refugees** moved to many places. Some traveled to the far north of Guatemala, in the Petén region. This area was more peaceful than other parts of Guatemala. Other refugees moved to Mexico, Belize, and the United States.

After the war ended, Guatemala had many problems. The economy was weak. Few people had jobs. Many cities had been damaged during the war. As a result, Guatemalans continued to leave the country.

Today, more than one million Guatemalans live outside of Guatemala. Many of them maintain close ties to their homeland. They often send money to their relatives. This is an important source of income for some families in Guatemala.

In 2014 alone, more than $5.5 billion came into Guatemala from relatives living elsewhere. Families who receive the money use it to buy food, clothing, and medicine. Sometimes the money goes to larger projects, such as building clinics and schools.

CHAPTER 4

PEOPLE AND CULTURES

These girls live in a traditional Mayan village on the banks of Lake Atitlán.

Many Guatemalans are of Mayan **descent**. Other Guatemalans have European roots. They are often of Spanish or German descent. Some Guatemalans are a mix of European and Mayan roots. They are called *Mestizos or Ladinos*.

About 60 percent of Guatemalans speak Spanish. It is the country's official language. More than 20 different Maya languages are also spoken in Guatemala. Of those languages, there are 100 different **dialects**.

The majority of Guatemalans are Roman Catholic. Guatemala has an important Catholic site in Esquipulas. The church there has a statue of Jesus that was carved in 1594. It is made of dark wood and draped in white satin robes. Each year, many people travel to see the statue. It is the most important Catholic shrine in Central America.

During Easter week, Catholics in Guatemala create designs leading to churches. People make the designs with stencils and colored sawdust.

Catholics in Guatemala celebrate many holidays. At Christmas, they have *posadas*. This holiday starts nine days before Christmas. During that time, people act out the Bible story of Mary and Joseph looking for an inn. People carry statues of Joseph and Mary through the streets.

The people knock on doors and ask for *posada* or lodging. They finally find a place to stay. The people enter the home. They eat traditional food, punch, and cookies.

Guatemalans also celebrate All Saints' Day. It is on November 1. They fly giant kites in the cemeteries. The kites symbolize the souls

of the dead going to heaven. The traditional feast includes *fiambre*. It is a salad of meat, fish, and vegetables.

Another holiday is Independence Day. It is on September 15. It marks Guatemala's independence from Spain. Guatemalan flags fly across the nation. Marching bands play traditional marimba music. People recite the national anthem. Children parade through the city in a drum procession.

On All Saints' Day, Guatemalans visit cemeteries and fly large, circular kites called *barriletes*.

A hero of Guatemala's independence was María Dolores Bedoya. In 1821, she ran through the streets of Guatemala with a lantern. It was a symbol of hope for Guatemala's future. Today, marathon runners carry on the tradition.

FUN FACT

ONE WORLD, MANY COUNTRIES

GUATEMALA Q0.05 aéreo

Today, the Maya make up about half of Guatemala's population. The mountains in western Guatemala have the largest population of Maya. They make up about 75 percent of the people who live in this area.

CHAPTER 5

DAILY LIFE

Homes are built into the hills outside of Guatemala City.

Daily life in Guatemala differs for wealthy and poor people. Wealthy Guatemalans have large homes. They have running water and electricity. Televisions, telephones, and computers are common.

Poor Guatemalans have small, simple homes. Houses have metal roofs and walls. The floors are often made of concrete. Many homes do not have running water or electricity.

In the cities, most people dress in clothing similar to that worn in the United States. Some Maya women wear traditional clothing. This includes a long skirt and a cotton blouse called a *huipil*.

Transportation in Guatemala is limited. Road conditions are poor. A common way to travel is by *camionetas*. They are colorful school buses. *Camionetas* do not have a set schedule and they can get quite crowded.

Soccer is the favorite sport in Guatemala. People mountain bike or climb the volcano in Antigua. Near the

Camionetas are old American school buses. The buses are exported to Guatemala, where they receive fresh paint and serve as public transportation.

coast, Guatemalans enjoy water sports. White-water rafting and kayaking are popular, too.

In Guatemala, lunch is the main meal of the day. It is bigger than the other meals. Common foods include corn tortillas, beans, and rice. *Frijoles* are black beans. They are a staple in many Guatemalan dishes. *Empanadas* are fried dumplings that are filled with meat or potatoes. *Chiles rellenos* are peppers stuffed with vegetables, meat, and cheese.

Children play a pickup game of soccer in Santiago Atitlán.

Money impacts all aspects of daily life. Wealth allows Guatemalans the comforts of home, shopping, entertainment, and food. Poor Guatemalans continue to struggle to provide for their families.

Despite the Guatemala's troubles, it is a country with a proud history. Its ancient people built advanced cities. Today, Guatemalans draw strength from their past. They are working to make their country a strong, modern nation.

Riding in a dugout boat is a traditional way to travel over water in Guatemala.

DAILY LIFE FOR CHILDREN

Some Guatemalan children attend school. Students study mathematics, science, and social studies. Lessons are in Spanish.

Not all children are able to attend school in Guatemala. In the countryside, schools may be too far away. Parents might not be able to afford clothes and supplies. Often these children stay home and help with farm work.

The ancient Maya ate many foods that are still popular today. They made guacamole, salsa, and corn tortillas. They drank coffee and hot chocolate, though it did not have milk or sugar in it.

FUN FACT • ONE WORLD MANY COUNTRIES

GUATEMALA Q 0.05 aéreo

FAST FACTS

Population: 14.6 million

Area: 42,042 square miles (108,889 sq km)

Capital: Guatemala City

Largest City: Guatemala City

Form of Government: Constitutional Democratic Republic

Languages: Spanish and Maya languages

Trading Partners:
The United States, Mexico, China, and El Salvador

Major Holidays:
Easter, Christmas, All Saints' Day, Independence Day

National Dish: *Pepian* (A hearty stew of slow-cooked meats, vegetables, seeds, and nuts)

A mother takes a break from weaving to play with her son in Santa Catarina Poropo, Guatemala.

GLOSSARY

civil war (SIH-vuhl war) A civil war is a fight between two groups in the same country. Guatemala's civil war lasted 36 years.

descent (dee-SCENT) Descent describes the line of people from earlier generations. Many Guatemalans are of Maya descent.

dialects (DYE-uh-lekts) Dialects are forms of a language that have unique characteristics. The Maya language has many dialects.

economy (ih-KON-uh-me) An economy is how a country runs its industry, trade, and finance. Jade is important to Guatemala's economy.

exports (ek-SPORTS) When a country exports goods, it sells them to other countries. Guatemala exports many of its crops.

imports (ihm-PORTS) When a country imports goods, it buys them from other countries. Guatemala imports many goods.

plazas (PLA-zuhs) Plazas are open public areas with places to walk, sit, and shop. Plazas are common in Guatemala.

refugees (re-fyu-GEES) Refugees are people who leave their country to escape danger. Refugees left Guatemala during the civil war.

republic (ree-PUB-lick) A republic is a place where an elected official rules over the land and people. Guatemala is a republic.

tourism (TOOR-ih-zum) Tourism is the act of people traveling for pleasure. Tourism is important in Guatemala.

TO LEARN MORE

BOOKS

Croy, Anita. *Guatemala*. Washington, D.C.: National Geographic, 2009.

Menchú, Rigoberta. *The Honey Jar*. Toronto: Groundwood Books/House of Anansi Press, 2006.

Morrison, Marion. *Guatemala*. New York: Children's Press, 2005.

WEB SITES

Visit our Web site for links about Guatemala: **childsworld.com/links**

Note to Parents, Teachers, and Librarians: We routinely verify our Web links to make sure they are safe and active sites. So encourage your readers to check them out!

INDEX

climate, 10
clothing, 26

economy, 17–18

food, 6, 27

Guatemala City, 14–15

holidays, 22–24
homes, 25

language, 21

Maya, 5–7, 15, 20–21, 26

rain forests, 10
religion, 21–22

school, 29

Tikal, 15–16
transportation, 26

volcanoes, 9

wildlife, 11